Writer of the Plains

Writer of the Plains

A Story about Willa Cather

by Tom Streissguth

illustrations by Karen Ritz

A Carolrhoda Creative Minds Book

Carolrhoda Books, Inc./Minneapolis

To Marie-Christine, the only pioneer I know.

Thanks to Amy Gelman, my editor; to Susan Rosowski of *Cather Studies* and the University of Nebraska for her review of the manuscript; and to the Willa Cather Pioneer House and Museum of Red Cloud, Nebraska.

Text copyright © 1997 by Tom Streissguth
Illustrations copyright © 1997 by Karen Ritz

This book is available in two editions:
Library binding by Carolrhoda Books, Inc.
Soft Cover by First Avenue Editions
c/o The Lerner Publishing Group
241 First Avenue North
Minneapolis, Minnesota 55401 U.S.A.

Library of Congress Cataloging-in-Publication Data

Streissguth, Thomas, 1958–
    Writer of the plains : a story about Willa Cather / by Thomas
Streissguth ; illustrations by Karen Ritz.
        p.   cm. — (Carolrhoda creative minds book)
    Includes bibliographical references (p.   ) and index.
    Summary: A biography of the American author Willa Cather,
emphasizing her youth and early career but covering all of her life.
    ISBN 1-57505-015-3 (lib. bdg.)
    ISBN 1-57505-060-9 (pbk.)
    1. Cather, Willa, 1873–1947—Biography—Juvenile literature.
    2. Cather, Willa, 1873–1947—Childhood and youth—Juvenile
literature. 3. Women novelists, American—20th century—Biography—
    Juvenile literature. [1. Cather, Willa, 1873–1947. 2. Authors, American.
    3. Women, Biography.] I. Ritz, Karen, ill. II. Title. III. Series.
PS3505.A87Z865   1997
813'.52—dc20
    [B] ·   96-27244

Manufactured in the United States of America
1 2 3 4 5 6 – JR – 02 01 00 99 98 97

Table of Contents

(1) Westbound Train

Willa Cather was standing on the long, rough boards of the station platform. Her father, mother, two brothers, and sister were nearby. Grandmother Boak was there, too, and so was Margie Anderson, the daughter of one of the Cathers' servants, along with her brother Enoch. They were all peering down the tracks, watching for the westbound train.

A few minutes later, the train slowly rumbled through, stopped, and waited. Willa stood back, minding her suitcase and taking in the scene. There were hisses of steam from the train, laughter and talk from strangers standing near the station house. Across the tracks, a series of soft, green hills rose above Back Creek Valley.

This was her home, and she might never see it again. Charles and Virginia Cather were leaving Virginia and bringing their family a thousand miles away, to the west, with everything they owned. Charles's father and his brother, George, had left the valley years ago to find better land to farm. Now Charles and his family would follow them.

Willa was nine. She had never traveled more than a few miles from her room in a three-story brick house called Willow Shade. The house had tall, white columns at the entrance and steep steps that brought visitors to the front door. Back Creek ran past an old mill that stood behind the house. Willa had spent many long afternoons playing in the fields and woods along the creekside.

She was the oldest child in her family, and she liked to play alone outside. But she liked to talk in company, too, and she could hold her own with any group of adults. She liked to play games with their names and with their serious adult talk. She could even make fun of them with a hidden joke or a sentence turned inside-out.

Charles Cather was proud of Willa, his first child. He was an easygoing farmer who grew crops and raised a small herd of sheep. When she was little, Willa liked to ride on her father's shoulders as he brought the sheep back into their pen at night. Vic, the Cathers' sheepdog, would gallop alongside the herd. As Willa watched and listened, Vic ran and barked to keep the sheep from going astray.

The Cathers had lived in America for six generations. They had been farmers, soldiers, and artisans. Jasper Cather, the first Cather in the New World, arrived from Wales in the 18th century. William Cather, Willa's grandfather, moved to Back Creek Valley in 1851. He had farmed 130 acres of land and built Willow Shade on his property. William and his wife, Caroline, raised two sons—Charles and George—and three daughters. A fourth daughter died in childhood.

Charles married Virginia Boak, a schoolteacher in Back Creek Valley. In 1873, their daughter Willa was born. In the same year, George Cather moved away from Virginia. The government was giving property away to people who agreed to settle on the land and farm it, and George had claimed land near the Republican River, in southern Nebraska. He received a homestead of 160 acres.

In their letters home to the family in Virginia, George and his wife described the frightening thunderstorms and cold, harsh winters of the plains. In summer, Nebraska's hot sun turned the soil into dust and the prairie grasses to dry stalks. Rainfall was scarce and hard to predict. After a drought, clouds of hungry grasshoppers sometimes destroyed the Cathers' crops.

But George also described Nebraska's fertile soil and open, unfenced land. Corn grew eleven feet tall, with ears more than a foot long. Plenty of free land was available, and a hardworking farmer could make it productive.

The Cathers in Virginia saw little opportunity where they lived. There was no open land in Back Creek Valley. There were no more fields to break or homesteads to build. If the price of crops and livestock fell, the farmers suffered. In 1874, Willa's grandparents followed George Cather to the Great Plains.

That was nine years ago. Now another generation of Cathers were boarding a westbound train. The whistle screamed as the train chugged out of the station, leaving Willow Shade behind. At the window, Willa again heard a dog barking. She saw Vic in a distant field, running hard with the train, trying to catch them. It was the last sight she had of Back Creek Valley.

②

The Empty Land

The train pulled into the Red Cloud depot and came to a stop. Billowing steam from the engine's smokestack floated over the flat, dusty ground. Tired, from the long journey, the Cathers stepped from the train with their bags and boxes. They climbed into the wagon that would take them to their new home.

As the wagon bounced over the uneven ground, Willa could see treeless fields on either side, stretching far into the distance. In front were deep ruts left by other wagons on the road ahead. The land was like nothing Willa had seen before. There were no green hills here. No fences marked the land, and no houses or barns could be seen. There were no people or horses. There were only crickets singing in the grass and birds flying in an enormous blue sky. Nebraska seemed empty.

The wagon pulled up to her grandfather's house. Around the house was the town of Catherton, proudly named by George Cather himself. But Willa could see that Catherton wasn't really a town. It was just a few farms, spread out far and wide over the prairie. Looking at it, Willa grew sad and homesick.

Her grandparents had gone back to visit Virginia. The Cathers settled into the house, which would be a temporary home. Willa had only a small cot to sleep on at night. During the day, she roamed over the fields on her grandfather's pony and explored the country with her brothers. One interesting spot was the Republican River, just two miles away to the south. The willows and cottonwoods that grew along the river were the only trees in sight. Willa liked to wade across the shallow water to the sandbars in the middle of the stream.

Soon the family settled in, and Willa began to visit her new neighbors. Many of them had made a much longer journey—all the way from Bohemia, Germany, or Norway. They had read about this land in pamphlets printed by the Burlington Railroad Company. The company wanted immigrants to settle along the tracks it had laid between Omaha and Denver.

Many of these Europeans were struggling to survive on this harsh frontier. They broke acres of sod, built their houses from the earth, borrowed the money to buy seeds, and then prayed for rain. They were homesick, poor, and often hungry.

Willa listened intently to the stories of these hardy pioneers. She had never before heard foreign languages or singing accents like theirs. They told her about their old homes, in the old countries. They also liked to tell stories about each other. Willa often heard about the Sadileks of Bohemia.

Francis Sadilek had been a violinist in Prague, the biggest city in Bohemia. He had come all the way to Nebraska to start his life over again. But he soon found that he couldn't make a living from growing crops. His family grew lonely and desperate. They were too poor to return to Bohemia.

One night, Mr. Sadilek picked up his shotgun, saying he was going to hunt rabbits. He went out to the barn, set his shotgun on the floor, and aimed it at his head. He pulled the trigger with his toe.

Willa always remembered that story. Like Mr. Sadilek, she missed her home. On cold winter days, she felt desperate, too. Now she had to live in Nebraska, at the end of the world, and she would probably never see Back Creek Valley or Virginia again. Someday, she thought, she might die right here, alone, in an empty cornfield.

③
William Cather, M.D.

After a year and a half, Charles Cather decided to give up farming. He sold his farming tools, his land, and all his livestock. He set up a small business in Red Cloud, making loans and selling insurance. Willa's father did not want to depend on the land and the weather to support his family.

Red Cloud was near the border of Nebraska and Kansas. It was named for a famous Indian chief. Eight times a day, trains running between Chicago and Denver stopped here to let out passengers and take on supplies. Many weary travelers left the train to stroll along the main street, where farmers and townspeople mingled on the dusty streets and rough wooden sidewalks.

In town, Willa went to school every weekday, something she hadn't always done when the family lived on the farm. She wanted to appear serious, so she wore trousers and a derby hat and cut her hair short, like a boy's. Sometimes she went out of the house with a wooden cane. People easily recognized her as she passed.

When school was out, she spent afternoons wandering along the Republican River. In the evening, she read in the downstairs parlor. Or she would call on her neighbors the Wieners. They had a big library of novels, stories, and poetry. Some of the books were translated from foreign languages.

Willa read dozens, even hundreds of books. Late at night, when the other Cathers were falling asleep, she read in her attic room. She liked the stories of Edgar Allan Poe, the novels of Charles Dickens, and the plays and poems of William Shakespeare. She loved *Anna Karenina,* a long novel about an unhappy family. She also liked Mark Twain's *Huckleberry Finn,* even though adults disapproved of it. These stories had strong characters, conflicts, and excitement.

She began collecting her own library. Willa carefully labeled her books with "Private Library" inside the cover and gave each book a number. She also wrote down her name—sometimes as "Willa Cather," sometimes as "William Cather, M.D."

For Willa had decided to become a physician. She

made friends with two doctors in Red Cloud. Dr. McKeeby, who tended the Cathers, sometimes brought her along on house calls. She also knew Dr. Damerall. One day, Dr. Damerall had to amputate a boy's leg. Willa helped by giving the patient chloroform, which made him pass out.

This was not ordinary behavior for a Red Cloud girl. Many townspeople believed that sons, not daughters, should have an interest in science and medicine. It was proper for young ladies to learn cooking, sewing, and housekeeping. They might also write poetry in their spare time. But it wasn't proper to wear trousers or to help doctors give chloroform to boys.

Willa went her own way. She didn't write stories of her own, but books fascinated her. She also loved plays and the theater. Whenever a professional theater company came through town, she hurried down to the station to watch the actors and actresses bustle on the platform.

The Cather siblings sometimes put on their own plays in the attic of their house. Willa also starred in her own productions in the Red Cloud Opera House, which was above a hardware store. In 1888, she put on *Beauty and the Beast,* playing the part of Beauty's father. The Red Cloud *Chief,* the town newspaper, gave the play a good review.

But as Willa grew older, she grew restless. Nothing much ever happened in Red Cloud, and the people in town led very ordinary lives. Willa walked their streets in her derby hats, quoted to them from books and plays she read, and looked them straight in the eyes as she spoke. She could feel that many of them didn't like her much. But she wouldn't change herself to suit them.

In June 1890, Willa graduated from high school with the other members of her class—two boys. The boys were going to work, but Willa didn't want to do that. And she didn't want to get married and settle down in Red Cloud. Instead, she would leave town to study medicine.

Her father borrowed money to send her to the University of Nebraska. That fall, she packed her bags and left home on an eastbound train for Lincoln, the state capital. She was happy to leave Red Cloud behind.

(4)
Strong Opinions

In a few hours, the train carried Willa to Lincoln. She spent her first days there walking around town, discovering stores, libraries, and two theaters. The University of Nebraska was on the north side of town. A tall iron fence surrounded the open, grassy campus and the university's four red-brick buildings.

Willa signed up for courses in science, math, and chemistry—subjects that doctors had to know. She also took courses in English, Greek, Latin, and rhetoric (the study of public speaking). She collected a small library in her room and took as many courses in literature as she could.

She soon found that the English classes were the best of all. The professors were as excited about novels and poetry as she was. Even better, Willa and the other students had to write long essays and defend their opinions in class.

She made friends with teachers, students, and towns-people. Many of her friends were writers. Dr. Julius

Tyndale wrote reviews for the *Lincoln Evening News.* Charles Gere owned the *Nebraska State Journal.* Herbert Bates was an English teacher who had come to Nebraska from Harvard, an important Eastern university.

Willa talked about books she had read and heard of many others that she wanted to read. It was fun to argue in class and duel with the other students. Few of them could keep up with her, and even fewer could argue with what she wrote. Writing an essay or a review always gave Willa the last word.

One day, Professor Ebenezer Hunt assigned Willa's class a paper on Thomas Carlyle. This Scotsman was a writer whom many people disliked. He was a conservative who was against voting rights for ordinary citizens. Willa thought Carlyle was misunderstood, and she wrote an essay that said so. She worked long hours trying to get the sentences and paragraphs just right. Finally, she turned the paper in and began studying for another assignment.

Professor Hunt read Willa's paper carefully. He then showed it to his friend Charles Gere, the publisher of the *Journal.* The beautiful writing style impressed both men. Gere decided to publish it in a Sunday edition of the *Journal.*

Willa didn't even know the *Journal* was printing

her essay until she opened the paper that day. There were her words—every line she had written in beautiful, straight lines and tall columns of type. Everyone else who opened the *Journal* that day could read them, and so could the readers of the *Hesperian,* the student newspaper.

The sight of her own writing fascinated her. She read the essay over and over, going back to the parts she liked. Finally, she read the initials beneath the printed columns—"W.C." Thousands of strangers were seeing those initials, too. They might like the essay. They might be wondering about her. They might be agreeing with her, or disagreeing.

Willa soon forgot about being a doctor.

She began writing stories, using memories to make up the plots and characters. She wrote a story called "Peter" about the suicide of her old neighbor Francis Sadilek. Professor Bates read "Peter" and sent it to a Boston magazine, *The Mahogany Tree.* The magazine published the story in May 1892. Willa was still only eighteen years old.

Her writing began to attract attention. In the fall of 1893, the *Nebraska State Journal* invited her to write regular columns. Will Owen Jones, the paper's managing editor, asked for one thousand words each time. Willa could write about anything or anybody.

She was still an unknown college student, so Jones wouldn't print her name. But he would pay her one dollar for each column. He called the column "One Way of Putting It."

Readers liked the columns. Jones began illustrating them with artists' drawings. Later, the paper printed a box around the headlines to set Willa's column off from the other stories. Finally, in May 1894, Jones agreed to print Willa's name above her columns. He allowed her to name the column, so she called it "As You Like It," later renaming it "The Passing Show."

That spring, Willa began reviewing plays that were presented at Lincoln's theaters. She loved going to plays, but she hated bad performances. She wasn't shy about criticizing actors, directors, and play-wrights. She wrote down the gossip she heard about them and happily gave her opinion of their talent.

Willa's reputation as a critic spread to other cities and states. She made Will Owen Jones proud, but she made performers nervous. They feared her sharp pen and were terrified of getting one of her bad reviews. She had strong opinions about novelists, too. She disliked many writers of her own time and found most women writers silly and sentimental.

In June 1895, Willa graduated from the university. Later that year, she went back to Cedar Street in Red

Cloud. Fall and winter came. There was no job in town for her, and little to do. She still wrote columns for the *Journal,* and also some articles for the *Courier,* a rival Lincoln paper. But these papers had no full-time position open for her. To pay for anything, she had to borrow money from her father.

Spring dragged on, and nothing happened. Willa wrote more columns while she dreamed of the train ride that would someday take her out of Nebraska. She would go to Chicago or even New York, where she could make a living doing what she wanted.

Finally, in June, she had some luck. A Mr. Axtell, who published a magazine called the *Home Monthly,* had read some of Willa's columns. Axtell needed a new managing editor for his magazine and offered Willa the job.

Willa would have to review every word the *Home Monthly* published, write much of the magazine on her own, and get it out on time. She would also have to move to Pittsburgh, where Axtell had his offices. She didn't know anyone in Pittsburgh. But she would be moving east, to a big city far from the plains, and supporting herself with a job and a salary. In a few days, she packed her bags and again left Red Cloud.

⑤

Names, Dates, and Dry Facts

Pittsburgh wasn't far from Back Creek Valley. Like Willa's Virginia home, it was set among green hills and steep valleys. But Pittsburgh was a big industrial city with huge steel plants. The plants worked around the clock to make steel.

Suddenly Willa was a long way from home. She was amazed by the smoke, dust, and noise of the city's mills and factories. Pittsburgh was all business, and all it seemed to care about was money and success. And the people here were strict about going to church, dressing right, and doing things the proper way.

Willa found a room in a boardinghouse and settled down in her new job. At the offices of the *Home Monthly,* Willa took charge. She decided what stories to publish, and how long they would be. There were empty columns and pages to fill, and filling them was her responsibility. She used many different names for the articles she wrote. An advice column was cred- ited to a woman named Helen Delay—that was really

Willa. The column advised people on the best books to read.

Most of *Home Monthly's* readers were housewives, so the magazine ran articles on housekeeping, cooking, and gardening. Willa didn't like the way the articles were written. But she had to edit them and try to make them as interesting as possible. It was hard work, and she grew bored with it. She cared more about writing her own stories for the magazine.

The *Home Monthly* printed Willa's short stories under many different pen names. She signed the name John Easton to the story "My Little Boy"; the story "The Princess Baladina" she signed Charles Douglass. One of her better stories, she thought, was "Tommy, the Unsentimental," about a student who travels east to college but who misses her life in Southdown, on the plains of the west. Willa signed "Tommy, the Unsentimental" with her own name.

In the summer of 1897, the Axtells sold the *Home Monthly* to a new owner. Willa had gone back to Nebraska for the summer. She decided to return to Pittsburgh and look for another job. By now, many editors and publishers in Pittsburgh knew her name and her writing. The publisher of the Pittsburgh *Daily Leader* offered her a job. She would review plays for a salary of seventy-five dollars a month.

Willa accepted the offer, but a few days after she started, another chance came her way. The paper's telegraph editor had quit. The *Leader* needed a temporary replacement until another man could be hired permanently.

Willa wanted to try this job, although she knew it was a hard one. She would have to quickly rewrite stories that came into the office by telegraph. They were up-to-the-minute stories about wars and disasters, about elections and crimes and sports. Often, the stories were too short, or incomplete. The telegraph editor had to fill in missing information, write a headline for the story, and have it ready fast.

Telegraph editors were men, not women. Publishers thought men could better handle the hard work and stress. They also thought men knew more than women about politics and current events. But Willa decided to ask for the job on a permanent basis anyway, and the *Leader's* publisher decided to hire her. She had proven herself, and he could pay her less than he would have to pay a man.

Telegraph editors worked afternoons and evenings. Willa sometimes worked all night, too, reading, writing, and rewriting. The telegraph reports were full of bad grammar and clumsy sentences, and she had to fix them. Writing headlines could be especially hard.

To get the reader's attention, the headlines had to be interesting. But many of the stories were about dull, everyday occurrences. There seemed no way to write something clever about them, but she had to try.

Hundreds of articles that Willa edited ran in the newspaper, though her name was not included in them. They appeared in all corners of the newspaper, sometimes on the front page, sometimes in the middle. Her words were read in a few minutes, then forgotten. When the readers were finished, they put the paper aside or threw it away.

Willa kept working at her columns and reviews, but she stopped writing stories for a time. It was too hard to concentrate on plots and characters. Instead, names, dates, and dry facts were taking all of her time. From her small office at the *Leader,* she saw a long road ahead, and she wasn't sure where it would take her.

6

A Tough Grader

Willa made many new friends in Pittsburgh. One of them was Isabelle McClung, the daughter of a wealthy judge. Miss McClung lived with her family in a big house in a fine neighborhood. She often invited Willa home for dinner. The two friends grew very close. In 1901, Isabelle invited Willa to live in the McClung house. Here Willa could live in comfort and work in peace and quiet. She happily accepted.

Willa worked at the *Leader's* offices downtown and wrote stories and reviews in her room at the McClungs'. She covered plays and concerts in Pittsburgh and New York and sent the reviews home to the Nebraska newspapers. The articles were filled with theater gossip and fascinating tales of actors, actresses, and nightlife. The readers back home could imagine for themselves the excitement of big cities and show business.

They might be imagining a glamorous big city life, but Willa was just tired. She was working, writing, and then returning to work. She was going out at night and not sleeping much. Friends came to visit, and there were dinners and meetings to attend.

At the offices of the *Leader,* Willa began to find the newspaper stories boring. The same stories seemed to keep happening, to the same people. There was no life or emotion in them. There was no skill to writing them.

Willa was tired of newspapering. In early 1900, she quit the paper and went to work for a weekly magazine called the *Library.* The paper published her poems, essays, and short stories. One of the essays was called "The Hottest Day I Ever Spent." "The Dance at Chevaliers" was a story about pioneers in Nebraska.

After six months, Willa was out of a job again. The owner of the *Library* had run out of money. In the spring, she took a job as an English teacher at Central High School. She could sleep at night and write during the summer months, when school was on vacation.

Miss Cather's classes were hard. In her English classes, students had to write a theme in the first few minutes of the class. They had to read a lot of books and write long papers. Willa was a tough grader who criticized poor writing. If she didn't like a paper, she might read it aloud in class and make fun of it.

Every June, summer vacation began. Willa usually went home to Nebraska. She stayed with her family and saw her friends. Back on the plains, she could watch the pioneers and farmers who were turning the raw land into neat, orderly fields and pastures.

In the summer of 1902, Willa decided to sail to Europe with Isabelle and another friend. They wanted to see all the towns and places they had been reading about in their books. Willa still remembered the pioneers she had known in Nebraska, and now she would have a chance to see their European homelands.

The three friends traveled to London. Then they crossed the English Channel for France. In the French countryside, she walked in narrow dirt lanes, watching farmers work their fields of wheat. Tall poplar trees lined the roads, forming a long green wall that waved slowly in the breeze. In one of the fields, Willa caught sight of an old, American-made harvesting machine. Years ago, when she was living in Red Cloud, she had ridden on the very same kind.

The sunny, warm day, and the sight of farmers working in their fields, reminded her of summers long ago in Nebraska. A pang of homesickness caught her, making her impatient to go home.

(7)

Telling the Truth

Writing and working for a living was hard going.
After teaching all day, Willa was too tired to take
notes or sketch outlines for her stories. Instead, she
had to grade papers and plan her lessons. She was not
reaching her goal of making a living as a writer, and
she often felt discouraged.

In January 1903, an offer came to publish a book of
her poetry. The publisher was Richard Badger of
Boston. Badger discovered young or unknown au-
thors and then offered to publish their works. But
unlike most publishers, Badger asked writers to help
pay for printing and binding the books.

Willa accepted Badger's offer anyway. She was
eager to see her words in a book, instead of in a magazine or a newspaper. She picked out thirty-eight of
her poems. Eleven of them had already been printed
in magazines. The others had not been published.
She named the book *April Twilights.*

The book didn't sell many copies, but Willa earned some good reviews from papers in New York and Chicago. She was proud of the book for a while. But much later in her life, when she read the poems again, she found them silly and embarrassing. She bought every copy of *April Twilights* she could find, took the copies home, and burned them.

At about the same time, a publisher named S. S. McClure was hearing about Willa Cather. McClure lived and worked in New York City. He owned *McClure's* magazine, and he also published books. His cousin, H. H. McClure, had once passed through Lincoln and had paid a visit to Will Owen Jones. The two men talked about writers they knew, and Jones praised the young woman who wrote columns for the *Journal.*

S. S. McClure was always looking out for new writers. After hearing about Willa, he invited her to submit some stories to his magazine. When he had read them, he sent her a telegram asking her to come to New York for an interview.

Several famous journalists worked at *McClure's.* Lincoln Steffens was a celebrity in New York. Ida Tarbell was one of the few women journalists working for a national magazine. Along with other writers for *McClure's,* they wrote articles about corrupt politicians and businesses. They wanted to improve society by revealing the wrongdoing of powerful people. Because they dug up a lot of dirty, unpleasant secrets, they were called "muckrakers."

Willa Cather didn't much care for muckraking journalism. She wrote stories. To her, a work of fiction was far more interesting than an article about a big-city mayor or a rich oil tycoon. A story could be like a painting or a symphony. It was made by the imagination, not by facts and figures. It was another way of telling the truth.

Still, if she could land a job at *McClure's,* it would mean moving to New York, the center of the publishing world. S. S. McClure himself had many friends in the business who could help her. It would be a way for her to publish her books, earn more reviews, and win an audience for her works.

In May, Willa arrived at the offices of *McClure's.* It was a bustling, noisy place. Office clerks rushed between the desks carrying papers and messages. Writers gathered around the desks to gossip. In the back of the large room was a door leading to McClure's office.

As Willa entered the publisher's office, McClure rose quickly from behind a crowded desk. He was a small, talkative man who seemed unable to keep still.

He shook hands with Willa and tried to put her at ease. He told her how he had traveled all over Europe and North America, searching for good writers for his magazine. He had found many including Mark Twain, Walt Whitman, and Sir Arthur Conan Doyle, who wrote the Sherlock Holmes stories. McClure knew them and had read all their works.

Willa tried to remain businesslike. She spoke about growing up in Virginia and Nebraska. She described her reviews and stories, and her small book of poetry. Then she listened closely as McClure explained his many plans for her future. He had no position for her, but from now on, he would publish anything she sent or find another publisher for it. Someday, he would also bring out a book of the stories she would write for McClure's. Willa and McClure got along well.

Willa went back to Pittsburgh. *McClure's* had inspired her to work harder on her short stories. McClure soon published "The Sculptor's Funeral," in which Willa described a famous artist who dies. According to the man's wishes, his body is returned to the small town in Kansas where he grew up, and where his old neighbors didn't think much of his career. *McClure's* also printed "Paul's Case." In this story, a young man from Pittsburgh yearning for big-city life steals from his boss to go to New York.

The name Willa Cather became familiar to the thousands of people who read *McClure's* and other national magazines such as *McCall's* and *Harper's*. In 1905, McClure published a collection of Willa's stories called *The Troll Garden*. "A Wagner Matinee" and six other stories were included.

This time, the reviews were mixed. *The Reader* called Willa's writing "vivid, strong, true, and original." But the *New York Times* said she was "too ambitious." The *Bookman* called the book a collection of "freak stories." Yet Willa was gaining the attention of many major newspapers. And S. S. McClure's interest in her continued. In 1906, when McClure finally offered Willa a job at his magazine, she gladly accepted.

New York was noisy and exciting, dusty and crowded and spectacular. It seemed like the center of the world. Willa had found a new hometown, one that she didn't want to leave.

Willa's first writing assignment came that fall. *McClure's* had a long manuscript by a writer named Georgine Milmine. It was a biography of Mary Baker Eddy, the founder of the Christian Science Church.

The manuscript was in bad shape. It was disorganized and full of spelling and grammatical errors. Names, dates, and places were wrong. Willa would have to edit the manuscript again, check all its facts, and rewrite the book for publication in the magazine.

To do the research, she traveled to Boston, the home of Mary Baker Eddy and Christian Science. Willa interviewed many people and spent long days in the Boston library, studying hundreds of dusty newspaper clippings. Instead of inventing plots and characters, Willa found herself taking thousands of notes on names and dates and events. Then she spent months correcting and revising the manuscript. Finally, *The Life of Mary Baker G. Eddy* was ready. The book ran in fifteen straight issues of *McClure's,* under Georgine Milmine's name.

Willa wanted no credit for the work, and she received none. It was just as well, because the book created a scandal. It showed many of the legends about Mary Baker Eddy to be false. Members of the Christian Science Church bought up all the copies of *McClure's* they could find and destroyed them. They stole copies from some libraries. At others, they simply scissored articles out of the magazine.

Willa was just glad the assignment was over. She hated the difficult, boring task of research and disliked rewriting someone else's work. But in Boston she had made many new friends. One of them was Sarah Orne Jewett, an author from Maine. Miss

Jewett's best known book was a collection of short stories called *The Country of the Pointed Firs.*

Miss Jewett had grown up in South Berwick, a small fishing village in Maine. She had spent many days at the seaside, listening to sailors and fishermen tell their tales of adventure. Her father had been a doctor, and she often accompanied him on his rounds. She heard many stories from the villagers, just as Willa had heard stories from the settlers near Red Cloud.

Willa and Sarah Orne Jewett became fast friends. In the fall of 1908, after her work on Mary Baker Eddy was finished, Willa traveled north to visit South Berwick. Miss Jewett received Willa in her house. Over the next few days, she gave Willa some advice about writing.

Willa was wasting her talent at *McClure's,* Miss Jewett said. It was impossible to work long hours at a magazine and write anything good at the same time. And Willa had lived enough and seen enough to write good books. She had known Nebraska when it was the frontier. It was a place that must have given her enough stories for a lifetime of writing. She had only to step away from her job and give herself enough time to write them.

Willa had often told herself the same thing. But how was she to step away, just like that, from her job?

And who wanted to read about Nebraska, a place so far from New York that it seemed to be a different country altogether?

Miss Jewett's advice repeated itself over and over to Willa as she rode the train back to New York.

8

S. S. McClure

The biography of Mary Baker Eddy caused a sensation. The story sold thousands of extra copies of *McClure's*. S. S. McClure rewarded Willa with a raise and a promotion. She was now the managing editor. She was responsible for deciding what stories ran in *McClure's* and what stories the magazine would reject. When McClure was away from the office, she would be the boss.

Her pay was better, but the work was harder. Hundreds of stories were arriving at her desk every month. She had to read them all and decide what to do with them. Most of them were uninteresting and badly written. In a short time, she began to hate the sight of words typed on manuscript paper.

S. S. McClure was happy with his new managing editor. She was hardworking and talented. She could repair a bad manuscript better than anyone he knew. She could find its good qualities and shape it into something he could publish and sell. Some day, he thought, she would make a fine reporter—as long as she didn't waste her time writing too much fiction.

McClure couldn't write himself. As he grew older, he thought about telling the story of his life in an autobiography. He asked Willa to help him as a ghostwriter. She would write the book under his name. Willa felt loyal to McClure for his help and friendship, and she agreed.

The two spent many long afternoons and evenings going over his past. As McClure remembered his boyhood, Willa carefully took notes. She organized his life into chapters, and then wrote out *My Autobiography,* by S. S. McClure. At the start of the book, McClure added a note thanking Willa for her help in the project.

After finishing *My Autobiography,* Willa moved on to write a new story. This one would be about a group of boys living on the plains of Nebraska...

It was late at night, on the last day of summer. The boys would spend this last night together before the new school year began. They sat on a sandbar in the middle of a shallow western river. The dying embers of a campfire threw a faint orange light on their faces.

Far to the southwest, in New Mexico, there was a tall red rock that nobody had climbed. The mysterious mesa was once the home of ancient cliff-dwellers.

There might be ruins there, or the bones and skulls of ancient inhabitants. No one knew. Someday, the boys vowed, they would make the journey to the mesa and climb its steep walls. Whoever reached the top first would tell the others about his discovery.

Many years pass. None of the boys ever reach the Enchanted Bluff. One becomes rich and prefers driving his new car to hiking or walking anywhere. Another teaches, leaving town and rarely coming back. Three boys stay in town and never leave. Another lives and dies in the back yard of the town's saloon. In their adult world, the Enchanted Bluff is no longer mysterious or even very interesting.

Following Miss Jewett's advice, Willa returned to her memories of Nebraska as she wrote this new story. For each character she imagined someone she had known, giving that memory a new name and words of her own. The story came easily, as the land and the people she had known came back to her.

Willa sold "The Enchanted Bluff" to *Harper's* magazine. Soon afterward, in 1909, Miss Jewett died. In the years that followed, Willa would often leave New York to stay in the house where Miss Jewett had lived, near the coast of Maine. She worked and read at Miss Jewett's desk, remembering the advice she had heard in the same room.

Willa took time off from *McClure's* and found enough quiet to work on a novel. In the fall of 1911, Willa's book was finished.

The story was about an engineer named Bartley Alexander. He has talent and ambition. He wins a job to design a long river bridge. But to save money, he must agree to use inexpensive, second-rate materials.

Alexander is a great success. But even as he wins the fame he always wanted, he is afraid of growing old and losing interest in his work. In England, he falls in love with a young actress he had known when he was younger. He leaves his wife, then returns home. One day, he learns his bridge is in danger of collapsing. He rushes to the site, but he arrives too late to save his creation. As the bridge fails, he plunges to his death.

Willa had a talent for remembering almost everything she had ever seen or read. She described London and England as she had seen it when she visited Europe with Isabelle McClung, and she used facts and details that she remembered from books and newspapers. In 1907, a bridge had collapsed in Canada. She used the accident as a model for her own book.

In her novel, Willa wanted to describe the problems that artists had. The best ones always wanted to create something better, something spectacular. But the strains of ambition were like the strains on a high, dangerous bridge. At any moment, disaster could strike.

Willa wasn't sure if her novel was any good. She knew *McClure's* would publish it if she asked them to, but she wondered if the magazine would accept it from a writer they didn't know. She tried to find out by putting the name Fanny Cadwallader on the title page. She sent the manuscript to a friend in St. Louis and had it mailed from there.

The trick didn't work. Willa had her style, and the editors at *McClure's* knew it well. And the name Fanny Cadwallader didn't seem quite real. They soon figured out who the author was, and *McClure's* ran *Alexander's Masquerade* in three parts in 1912.

A publisher then agreed to bring out the novel in book form. Willa changed the name to *Alexander's Bridge.* Some critics gave it good reviews, but Willa wasn't satisfied. When she read her words again, she was disappointed. Her characters didn't seem real. The book was too long, and the story was uninteresting. It seemed like a play, with fake walls, cardboard furniture, and actors reading lines. She didn't believe in it. She started again, this time writing about the people on the frontier. This time, the words came easily.

⑨

The Bohemian Girl

McClure's printed Willa's story "The Bohemian Girl" in 1912. It was a long story about immigrants living and struggling in Nebraska. It was very different from most stories that ran in *McClure's*. The magazine's readers were used to stories about artists and city people who lived among the wealthy. But many of these readers also liked "The Bohemian Girl."

The praise took Willa by surprise. She knew that "The Bohemian Girl" was better than *Alexander's Bridge.* The characters were people she knew and understood. Instead of carefully writing like Henry James, she just listened to her own voice and told the story in her own way.

She began working on another long story, about a pioneer farmer named Alexandra. This pioneer couldn't write or paint. But Willa saw her as an artist, one who could turn rough, empty land into a garden.

She wrote several thousand words of the story and was happy with them. But she couldn't think of a way to continue the story, or finish it. She stopped writing and put away the manuscript.

In the spring, she planned a trip to the Southwest to see her brother Douglass, who worked for the Santa Fe railroad. She stopped in Red Cloud, then headed for Denver and Albuquerque, New Mexico. From Albuquerque, she boarded a Santa Fe train to Winslow, Arizona. It was a small, dusty town surrounded by a hot desert. Douglass lived here when he wasn't working out on the rail lines.

The two Cathers stayed in a small wooden house with an English cook and a railroad brakeman named Tooker. Douglass thought that the house might be a good place for Willa to write. She had brought along the manuscript of "Alexandra" and would try to finish it if she could. But Winslow was a rundown and depressing place. Willa had no privacy and couldn't settle in. Not a single line came to her.

When Willa couldn't stand Winslow any longer, she and Douglass, along with Tooker, left to camp in the mountains of northern Arizona. They traveled by horse-drawn wagon to Walnut Canyon, where ancient Indians had made dwellings in the sides of the steep cliffs. They followed the tributaries of the Colorado River and walked along the rim of the Grand Canyon. For the first time, Willa was in a real desert.

Far from the lights and noise of New York, she had no work to do and plenty of time to think. Gradually her life came into sharp focus. Willa saw, finally, that she was wasting her time. She was spending her days rushing from one small task to the next, not seeing where she should go.

The desert air seemed to clear her mind of these worries. She decided she would go back to New York and forget the details and deadlines of magazines. Stories would take their place, and she would get them all down on paper.

On the way back east, Willa stopped in Red Cloud to see her friends and her family. It was June, the season of the early wheat harvest. The warm summer days were the same every year she went back. A hot sun shone over the fields and farmhouses, which floated like islands in a sea of prairie grass and corn.

She had an idea for a story set right here, in the countryside near a small town like Red Cloud. It would be about a jealous husband—an immigrant from Europe—and his young wife. At the Cather house, she began to write it. Her family let her work without interruptions.

Just before leaving Red Cloud, Willa finished the story. At the end, there is a killing in a field under a mulberry tree. On the first page, she wrote out the title of the story: "The White Mulberry Tree."

On the way back to New York, she stopped in Pittsburgh and stayed with the McClungs. In the quiet attic room where she had once lived, she pulled out the manuscript of "Alexandra" again. Willa read a few pages. It was a good story, but it had no ending. Somehow, she had to finish it.

Another idea then came to her. She would combine "Alexandra" and "The White Mulberry Tree." Both stories took place on the frontier, and both described immigrants who farmed the land. Alexandra would be the main character. Together, the two stories were just long enough for a novel.

She worked on the stories to make them run together more smoothly. She put the characters from "The White Mulberry Tree" into "Alexandra," which would make up the first half of the book. As a final part, Willa wrote out another description of Alexandra's life. These scenes take place long after the action of the main story. The story of the immigrants seems to become the reader's own distant memory.

The words came with no effort. Willa quickly finished the book and read it again from the beginning.

Many pages held no action at all—just description of people and places. And there was something awkward about the way she had put the two stories together. But it was an honest book. It was clear that the writer was telling the truth. Willa knew it was better than her first novel.

Willa borrowed the title *O Pioneers!* from a poem by Walt Whitman and wrote it across the title page. The book was published in June 1913 and earned many good reviews. Some critics were surprised by Miss Cather's strong characters and vivid descriptions. She could write well, they all agreed, even though she was a woman from Nebraska.

The trip to the Southwest had made up Willa's mind. She would work for herself now and write a few magazine articles, when necessary, to make ends meet.

Willa had accepted one more assignment from *McClure's*. She would write an article about three American singers. One of them was Olive Fremstad. She had been born in Sweden but raised in St. Peter, a small town in Minnesota. Now Fremstad was singing to audiences in concert halls all over the world. She had a strong, clear voice that carried into the back rows of the largest concert halls. Audiences adored her, and critics praised her.

Willa spent the next few weeks interviewing her subject and watching her performances. Miss Fremstad was a strong and temperamental person. She didn't always get along with stage directors, managers, and other performers, and she would fly into a rage over small details. Willa was fascinated. She saw the rough pioneer women of Nebraska, and a little of herself, in Olive Fremstad.

Before the assignment, Willa had already decided to write a book about an opera singer. She made Olive Fremstad the model for the book's main character, named Thea Kronborg. Instead of St. Peter, the singer in the book grows up in a place called Moonstone, Colorado. Willa added descriptions of the country she had seen in the Southwest. The character's childhood was based partly on Willa's own.

She went back to the McClung house in Pittsburgh, where she could settle down again in her old room. She wrote almost thirty thousand words in four weeks and finished the novel. She called this book *The Song of the Lark.* It was three times longer than *O Pioneers!*

There were some bad reviews for *The Song of the Lark.* Many critics thought Miss Cather had just written too much. The book was full of small details that seemed unimportant to the story. But Olive Fremstad herself had read the book during a journey to England. When she met Willa again, she praised the book and the description of herself. Her opinion made Willa feel a little better.

Willa quickly pressed on with another book. Traveling with her family, a young Bohemian girl named Ántonia arrives in the town of Black Hawk on the Burlington train. In Europe, Ántonia's father had made a good living from his work. But on the open plains, he fails. The family has nothing to eat and no idea of how to live from the land. They burrow into their sod house like prairie dogs in their holes.

Winter comes, and the family goes hungry. The land has defeated them. One cold night, Ántonia's father goes to the barn and lies down on a bench. Like Francis Sadilek, whose story Willa had heard long ago, he places a gun against his head and pulls the trigger with his toe.

After seeing her father buried, Ántonia moves to town and works as a servant for a family. The people of Black Hawk look down on her and on her friends. They have no education and, it seems, no future. They can't speak English very well, and they are from poor countries in Europe. The boys in town stay away.

One day, Ántonia meets a railroad worker. She falls in love and leaves town with him, but she soon returns. The man has deserted her, left her alone with a baby to raise. Later, she marries another man and raises a large family. Despite all her bad luck, she manages to be happy. Her house and family, and the land she lives on, are all she needs.

Willa wrote the book in the first-person voice. The voice belongs to a male character named Jim Burden. In the first pages of the book, he explains that he will tell the story of Ántonia as he remembers her. Because so many people didn't understand her, Burden wants to explain Ántonia himself. He calls his book "My Ántonia."

When *My Ántonia* came out in 1918, Willa earned praise from nearly every reviewer in the country. Many were happy to discover an American writer who had as much skill as the best writers from Europe.

With the success of this book, Willa finally had what she always wanted. Publishers would print her words, and millions of readers would open her books, eager for a fine story about the land and people of her imagination.

Afterword

Willa wrote many more books about people struggling with a changing world. Her own life changed little for the next thirty years. With a friend, Edith Lewis, she moved to an apartment in New York City's Greenwich Village. She wrote stories, essays, and novels, went to plays and concerts, visited friends, and traveled.

Gradually she grew unhappy with the society that she lived in and wrote about. Most people, it seemed to her, cared only for money, possessions, and comfort. There was nothing courageous about them. The pioneers who had made a living from the raw land were all dead and forgotten.

Over the next eighteen years, she wrote many novels, including *One of Ours, The Professor's House, Shadows on the Rock, Death Comes for the Archbishop, A Lost Lady,* and *Lucy Gayheart.* She had many fans, but the critics moved on to new writers and new styles. Willa's kind of storytelling grew out of fashion for a time. But later she became one of the most popular of all writers. Critics appreciate her again, and people all over the world read her books.

Willa went back to her earliest memories, in Back Creek Valley, for *Sapphira and the Slave Girl.* This novel, about the South and slavery, was her last, finished in 1940. She died in New York City in 1947.

Booklist

Selected works by Willa Cather:

The Troll Garden. New York: McClure Phillips & Co., 1905.
Alexander's Bridge. Boston: Houghton Mifflin Company, 1912.
O Pioneers! Boston: Houghton Mifflin Company, 1913.
The Song of the Lark. Boston: Houghton Mifflin Company, 1915.
My Ántonia. Boston: Houghton Mifflin Company, 1918.
One of Ours. New York: Alfred A. Knopf, 1922.
Death Comes for the Archbishop. New York: Alfred A. Knopf, 1927.
Sapphira and the Slave Girl. New York: Alfred A. Knopf, 1940.

Bibliography

Cather, Willa. *Early Novels and Short Stories.* New York: Library of America, 1987.

Gerber, Philip L. *Willa Cather.* Boston: Twayne Publishers, G. K. Hall & Co., 1975.

Lewis, Edith. *Willa Cather Living.* New York: Alfred A. Knopf, 1953.

O'Brien, Sharon. *Willa Cather: The Emerging Voice.* New York: Oxford University Press, 1986.

Robinson, Phyllis C. *Willa: The Life of Willa Cather.* Garden City, NY: Doubleday & Company, Inc., 1983.

Woodress, James. *Willa Cather: A Literary Life.* Lincoln, NE: University of Nebraska Press, 1987.

Index

64